CONTENTS

Words in **bold** are in the glossary.

Engineering inventions

Strange. Unusual. Odd. When people set out to create new inventions, they don't usually have these words in mind. But sometimes, interesting problems require surprising solutions.

Most people create products to solve problems. They make new things to make life easier and more enjoyable. They do this through the process of engineering. There are steps that help engineers come up with better products.

Engineers often make a computer model of their invention first.

WEIRD INVENTIONS

BY JENNIFER **KAUL**

Raintree is an imprint of Capstone Global Library Limited, a company incorporated in England and Wales having its registered office at 264 Banbury Road, Oxford, OX2 7DY – Registered company number: 6695582

www.raintree.co.uk
myorders@raintree.co.uk

Text © Capstone Global Library Limited 2021
The moral rights of the proprietor have been asserted.

Edited by Mandy Robbins
Designed by Kyle Grenz
Original illustrations © Capstone Global Library Limited 2021
Picture research by Kelly Garvin
Production by Kathy McColley
Originated by Capstone Global Library Ltd
Printed and bound in India

978 1 3982 0440 9 (hardback)
978 1 3982 0441 6 (paperback)

British Library Cataloguing in Publication Data
A full catalogue record for this book is available from the British Library.

Acknowledgements
We would like to thank the following for permission to reproduce photographs: Capstone Studio: Karon Dubke, left 9, 11, 13, 16, 18, 29, 31, 32, 33, 36, 37, 38, 42, 45; Getty Images: Alfred Eisenstaedt, 6, BEHROUZ MEHRI, 41, Culture Club, 15, James D. Morgan, 23, Mike McGregor, 25, Popperfoto, 21, Star Tribune via Getty Images, 34, Thomas S. England, 27; iStockphoto: xavierarnau, 26; Shutterstock: Aleksangel, (earbuds) 9, argus, (sparks) design element, Gorodenkoff, 4, Ivo Antonie de Rooij, 22, JGA, Cover, July Prokopiv, Cover, Kryvenok Anastasiia, 14, Marina Akinina, (headphones) 9, Martial Red, (watch) 9, Monkey Business Images, 43, Nikodash, 7, Ron and Joe, (hat) 9, SatrianiPh, Cover, selivanoff1986, Cover, vectorisland, (hat) 9, vectornetwork, (walkman) 9, Vitaly Korovin, 35, Yana Lesiuk, 1

Every effort has been made to contact copyright holders of material reproduced in this book. Any omissions will be rectified in subsequent printings if notice is given to the publisher.

All the internet addresses (URLs) given in this book were valid at the time of going to press. However, due to the dynamic nature of the internet, some addresses may have changed, or sites may have changed or ceased to exist since publication. While the author and publisher regret any inconvenience this may cause readers, no responsibility for any such changes can be accepted by either the author or the publisher.

The process of engineering

1. ASK
Ask questions about the problem and how it might be solved.

2. RESEARCH
Learn more about the problem and what products already exist.

3. IMAGINE
Imagine products that could help solve the problem.

4. PLAN
Plan which product to create.

5. CREATE
Create a prototype.

6. TEST
Test how well the prototype works to solve the problem.

7. IMPROVE
Repeat the engineering process to improve your inventions and build on the ideas of others.

Many products solve the problems they were meant to solve. These inventions become a part of our daily lives. Some are so bizarre that they're rarely used or never sold at all. Others find a place in shops because they're so unique or hilarious. And some strange inventions actually end up being useful.

Television goggles

Watching TV and films is very different now than it was in the 1960s. In the past, you had to watch a **stationary** TV and turn nobs to change channels. Inventor Hugo Gernsback wanted to change this by inventing television goggles in 1963.

Gernsback's teleyeglasses included a screen for each eye. They had a long TV antenna sticking out of the top, and they displayed tiny pictures.

The television goggles were featured in *Life* magazine in July of 1963. The article stated that Gernsback believed his invention was "a device for which . . . millions yearn". *Life* called it a "handy, pocket-size portable TV set".

Hugo Gernsback, 1963

Gernsback's television goggles may have helped inspire virtual reality goggles.

Today, you can stream TV shows and films on smartphones and tablets as well as TVs. You can choose what to watch and take your devices with you wherever you go. You can even put on a virtual reality headset to view media in 3-D.

Gernsback's television goggles failed to find success. A **prototype** of the device was made, but it was never sold. However, with today's portable devices and virtual reality headsets, maybe Gernsback was just ahead of his time.

Inventor turned author

Gernsback started magazines and wrote stories to advertise his products. Today, he is known for creating the genre called **science fiction**. The Hugo Awards are given to science fiction authors each year.

Portable radio hat

Do you like listening to music on the go? If so, you probably use a smartphone or MP3 player. But what if you had lived in the 1940s? Your only option would have been to wear a portable radio hat.

An early version of the radio hat was created in 1931. It combined a straw hat with a small built-in radio. This product never took off. But the idea interested a man called Victor Hoeflich.

Hoeflich created his own version of the radio hat in 1949. He called it the "Man-from-Mars Radio Hat". The top of the hat held tubes, a round antenna and the volume control. A thin wire connected the hat to a battery, which the wearer carried in his or her pocket.

Fact!

Hugo Gernsback was fascinated by the radio hat. One of his magazines, Radio-Electronics, even featured it on the cover.

Portable music players introduced through the years

- o 1931: straw radio hat, the first portable music invention
- o 1949: Man-from-Mars radio hat
- o 1979: Sony Walkman, a portable cassette tape player
- o 1984: Sony Discman, a portable CD player
- o 2001: Apple iPod, a portable MP3 player
- o 2015: Apple Watch, a wearable device that plays music

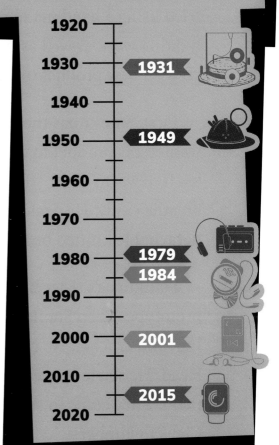

1920
1930 — 1931
1940
1950 — 1949
1960
1970
1980 — 1979
1984
1990
2000 — 2001
2010
2015
2020

A NEW KIND OF TOY ENTERTAINMENT
WITH GREAT GIFT APPEAL

the amazing NEW

Man-from-Mars
RADIO HAT

COMPLETE 2-TUBE RADIO BUILT INTO A HAT

Here's the two-tube topper you've read about in LIFE, TIME, BUSINESS WEEK, POPULAR SCIENCE, RADIO ELECTRONICS, and many other magazines and newspapers from coast to coast. Hundreds of picture stories and news items announcing the RADIO HAT have harvested truck-loads of inquiries and orders, from Miami to Seattle. "Exceptionally efficient receiver"... better than some 4-tube sets," says Hugo Gernsbach, Editor of Radio Electronics Magazine. Yes, the RADIO HAT is a wonderful dream-come-true . . . it's not only a great new toy, but a marvelous radio receiver.

$**7**^{95}
Retailing at plus fed. tax
Complete with Battery Pack

Study the amazing features, then WRITE TODAY. Learn how you can join the already great program for "Radio Hatting" America.

★ **Covers entire broadcast band within 20 miles**
★ **Set weighs 5 ozs., hat 7 ozs.**
★ **Conceals in lining ¼" thick**
★ **Absolutely mobile . . . no extra aerial needed**
★ **Volume and tone equal to many portables**
★ **Regulation waterproof sun helmet . . . adjustable size**

AMERICAN MERRILEI CORP.
918 HALSEY STREET • BROOKLYN 33, N. Y.

Several different kinds of radio hats were advertised in the 1930s and 1940s.

Knitted beard hat

David Stankunas had a problem. He loved snowboarding, but his chin always got cold. He tried using a bandana to solve this problem. But it didn't work as well as he hoped. He decided to create a new product to help solve his problem.

First, Stankunas thought about what he wanted his product to do. It needed to keep his face warm while still allowing him to breathe easily. He decided to make a hat with a **detachable** knitted beard.

Stankunas's sister helped him create a prototype. Then Stankunas taught himself to knit and crochet. He called his invention Beard Head. He started a website where he could sell them. They come in styles ranging from Santa Claus to lumberjack, for kids to sports fans.

With Beard Heads, you don't need to be able to grow a beard in order to have one.

Stankunas faced some challenges while working on his Beard Heads. One setback was a **lawsuit**. One of his competitors claimed to have a **patent** on a design he was using. Eventually, the competitor ended up dropping the charges.

Companies in court

Companies need to be careful when they create and sell new products. They need to make sure their products aren't too similar to the ideas of others. When it seems like someone may have copied another person's idea, they can get into legal trouble. This is called **infringement**. Companies can take their competitors to court over infringement. They do this to avoid losing customers and money. Those found guilty of infringement can be fined large amounts of money or be forced to stop making their product.

Stankunas also tried to find experts to help him on the US TV show *Shark Tank*. They chose not to work with him because they thought his product sounded like a **fad**. To make matters worse, the Beard Heads website crashed during the show.

Appearing on *Shark Tank* helped Stankunas's company. It resulted in more long-term sales. It helped spread the word about his product. And it helped him learn more about business, his product and himself.

The beard on the Beard Head can be attached and detached using buttons.

Dog jumper

If you're worried your dog might get
too cold outside, you might consider a dog
jumper. Many dogs grow thick fur before
winter. But small and short-haired breeds
may need more warmth than what nature
affords them. They need a dog jumper.

Dog jumpers help short-haired dogs
enjoy the outdoors on cold days.

A dog jumper is just what it sounds like – a jumper made for a dog. They come in different shapes and sizes for different breeds. They also come in many colours and styles for pet owners to choose from. There are hoodies, holiday jumpers, winter jackets and costumes. Some are plain. Others are whacky. There are even shops dedicated to pet fashion.

Fact!

It's important to make sure dogs stay safe in their clothes. Make sure dog jumpers fit comfortably, and avoid small parts that can be chewed off.

There are written records of dogs wearing clothes as early as the 1830s in Europe.

Grass sandals

Who doesn't love the feeling of fresh-cut grass under their feet? What if you could bring that feeling from your garden to the city, the beach or even the inside of your house?

Take the feeling of fresh grass beneath your feet to the swimming pool.

Grass sandals allow people to enjoy the soft feeling of fresh-cut grass beneath their feet everywhere they go. These flip-flops have a layer of fake green grass to cushion your feet. It has a similar look and feel to real grass. But being fake means the grass doesn't have to be watered, left out in the sun or mowed!

Grass sandals aren't made of natural materials. But they're made to be comfortable and unique. Grass sandals give you the feeling of walking barefoot with the protection of wearing shoes. They can be worn without worrying about stepping on something sharp on the ground. People can buy them or make their own using flip-flops and turf. So next time you dream of feeling the grass between your toes, a trip to a craft shop for sandal supplies might just do the trick!

Fact!

You can make your own grass sandals with the help of an adult. All you need are flip-flops, artificial grass turf, scissors and a hot glue gun.

Motorised ice cream cone

We can all agree that drippy ice cream is annoying. Sticky fingers and a soggy cone are gross. And no one wants to waste ice cream! So inventors created the motorised ice cream cone to help prevent these things from happening.

There are two versions of this invention. One includes a removable, dishwasher safe cup. The other allows you to insert your own edible cone. Both designs have a motor and a battery inside.

Scoop your ice cream right into the washable version of the motorised ice cream cone.

Inside a motorised ice cream cone

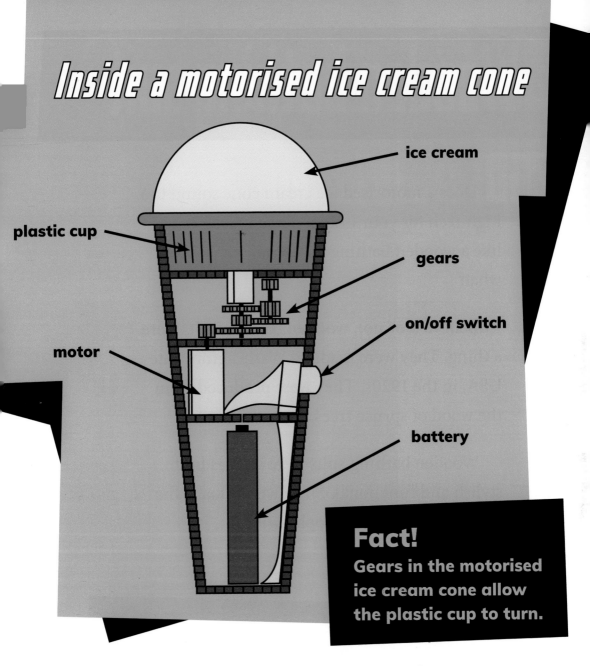

ice cream

plastic cup

gears

on/off switch

motor

battery

Fact!
Gears in the motorised ice cream cone allow the plastic cup to turn.

All you have to do is load it with ice cream, flick a switch and stick out your tongue! The motorised cone will rotate your ice cream. That way, you can eat it evenly without having to turn the cone yourself.

Wooden bathing suit

Does a motorised ice cream cone sound too high-tech for your liking? Then maybe you'd like a wooden bathing suit. Wait – a wooden what?

Believe it or not, wooden bathing suits were a thing. They were made in Washington State, USA, in the 1920s. They were produced from the wood of spruce trees.

Wooden bathing suits were seen as both stylish and functional. Since wood floats, the bathing suits helped people swim.

Fact!
Would you be willing to wear a wooden bathing suit? If not, you could always consider a bathing suit made out of bicycle tyres. That was another weird invention of the time.

Models called the "Spruce Girls" wore wooden bathing suits during "Wood Week". The event was meant to promote the area's timber industry. Timber is still an important part of Washington's economy.

A group of "Spruce Girls" pose in their wooden bathing suits.

Driving on land and in water

Can you imagine a car that floats? The Amphicar does! Amphicar is short for "**amphibious** car". It works both on the land and in the water.

Amphicars aren't a new idea. They were first developed for use in World War II (1939–1945). They were produced for the public from 1961 to 1965. Only about 3,800 were made. Few people purchased them because they were expensive.

The Amphicar stopped being sold because of new laws. The car didn't meet new safety regulations, and it created more pollution than was allowed.

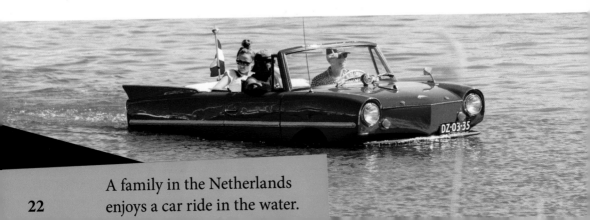

A family in the Netherlands enjoys a car ride in the water.

A driver in Australia takes his Amphicar from the road into the water.

Some people still own Amphicars. They enjoy the fun and convenience of driving their cars into the water. They like the strange looks they get when they pull up to riverside restaurants. There's even an International Amphicar Owners' Club. It holds Swim-ins around the United States.

Fact!
Past US presidents Lyndon B. Johnson and Jimmy Carter owned Amphicars. So did the singer Madonna.

Super Soaker

Have you ever drenched someone with a Super Soaker water blaster? This invention has started countless water fights. And it all started with a man called Lonnie Johnson.

Johnson enjoyed creating things. Growing up in Alabama, USA, his friends called him "the Professor". Johnson invented a robot in 1968, when he was in high school. He called it Linex. Johnson's Linex won first place at a science fair.

Johnson went on to graduate from university and began a career at the National Aeronautics and Space Administration (NASA). He worked on many projects there. One was a refrigeration system. He tested his invention by hooking up a nozzle to his bathroom sink. A stream of water shot into his bath. Johnson had accidentally created the basis of the Super Soaker.

Lonnie Johnson poses with the Super Soaker he invented for a photo shoot in 2010.

Many other company have created their own version of Johnson's Super Soaker.

Johnson knew he'd made something special. He worked to make the rest of the water blaster. Soon, he had a prototype. Johnson let his 7-year-old daughter test it out with her friends, and they loved it.

It took seven years for Johnson to find a company to **manufacture** and sell his product. It became available in 1990. Twenty million Super Soakers were sold in their first summer in shops.

Johnson designed many more versions of the Super Soaker. He also created some types of Nerf guns. He has over 100 patents to his name.

Johnson poses with a Super Soaker and his patent for the invention.

Singing medicine dispenser

If you're like most people, you probably don't look forward to taking your medicine. But would you change your tune if your medicine dispenser sang to you? Tiffany Krumins invented a singing medicine dispenser called Ava the Elephant®. It was featured on the TV show *Shark Tank* in 2009.

Krumins came up with her idea when she worked as a nanny. The child she looked after didn't like taking his medicine. To encourage him, she created a stuffed elephant head out of fabric and sponges. Inside was a medicine dropper and the sound chip from a greetings card.

Ava the Elephant is meant to help babies and toddlers take their medicine. It has a friendly face and plays soft music. The medicine comes out of the elephant's trunk.

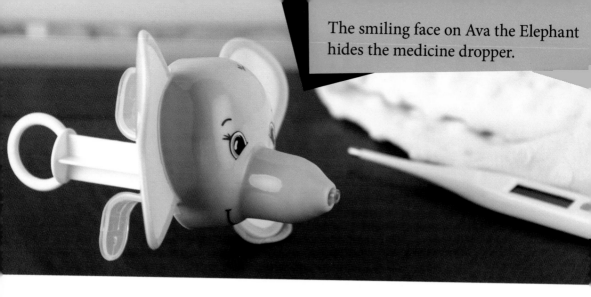

The smiling face on Ava the Elephant hides the medicine dropper.

Krumins also started a company called Mom Genius. She runs workshops and helps other inventors who are starting out. Many of the products she supports are for babies and children, including safety barriers for stairs and learning programmes.

Odd inventions for desperate parents

There are many strange products on the market for frustrated parents to choose from. One is the NoseFrida. It has a tube that can be placed in a baby's nose and is attached to a long straw. An adult sucks the baby's bogeys out through the straw, and they get trapped in the tube. Another product is the Baby Mop. This is an outfit for babies with microfibre mops on the arms and legs. When the baby crawls around on the floor, the floor gets cleaned!

Glow-in-the-dark toilet paper

Have you ever needed to go to the toilet in the middle of the night? The flash of the bathroom light can be too bright. But a night-light isn't always bright enough. Maybe it's time to consider glow-in-the-dark toilet paper!

Glow-in-the-dark toilet paper could be useful for late night toilet trips. It could help during camping trips and power cuts too. It could also be a funny joke gift to give a friend.

What makes the toilet paper and other glow-in-the-dark products glow? They contain phosphors. Phosphors give off light once they're energized. To get energized, the phosphors need to be exposed to light. This charges them. Then, when the product is placed in the dark, the phosphors make it glow.

With glow-in-the-dark toilet paper, you'll never
have to search for toilet paper in the dark again.   31

Post-it Watch

We all have a lot on our minds. Sometimes, it's hard to remember what we have to do each day. Never fear. Post-it Watches can save the day!

Post-it Watches can help you keep track of important appointments.

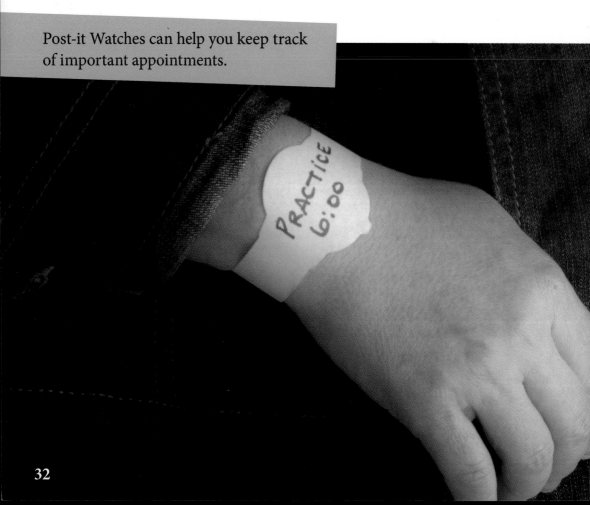

Post-it Watches are just like regular Post-it Notes, but they're shaped differently.

Post-it Watches are Post-it Notes that wrap round your wrist. A pad of these sticky notes looks like a watch lying flat. You can write what you need to remember on the face of the paper watch. Then you can wrap it round your wrist. One end is sticky, which helps the watch stay in place.

Post-it Watches can help you remember phone numbers, events and tasks you need to do. They can also be used for fun. You can decorate them with stickers, draw your own watch designs or write notes to friends.

Art Fry poses with Post-it Notes next to a billboard advertising the product he helped to invent.

A money-making mistake

Post-it Notes were actually invented by mistake at a company called 3M. The year was 1968. Dr Spencer Silver was trying to create a strong **adhesive**. But he accidentally made a weak one. It kept its stickiness and could be removed without damaging a surface.

At first, 3M wasn't sure what to make with the adhesive. Dr Silver waited five years for inspiration to strike. Luckily, another scientist at 3M called Art Fry had an idea. He needed a way to mark songs in a book when he sang in his church choir. The two scientists teamed up to create what was first called Press n' Peel. The name was later changed to Post-it Notes. Post-it Notes now come in many shapes and sizes. They are used in schools, offices and homes around the world.

Fact!

The yellow colour often used on Post-it Notes was an accident too. That just happened to be the colour of the paper scraps used to first test the product.

Jelly Belly beans

Do you like to eat dirt? What about bogeys and earwax? Hopefully your answer is no. Unless, that is, you get stuck with an unsavoury flavour from a batch of jelly beans.

The Jelly Belly company sells countless flavours of delicious jelly beans. They are also the home of Bertie Bott's Every Flavour Beans, based on J.K. Rowling's Harry Potter books. In the books, Bertie Bott is a sweetmaker. He invented Every Flavour Beans for the wizarding world.

Fact!

Jelly Belly now makes other sweets based on J.K. Rowling's Harry Potter books. These include chocolate frogs and jelly slugs!

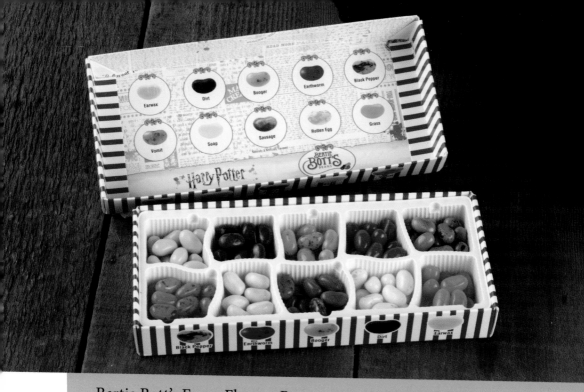

Bertie Bott's Every Flavour Beans comes with a key inside the box top, telling people which coloured bean is which disgusting flavour.

With J.K. Rowling's permission, innovators at Jelly Belly created these beans for the real world. The mix contains plenty of good flavours, including blueberry, green apple and marshmallow. But others taste like earthworms and vomit.

Pet Rock

Do you have a pet? If not, do you want one? Maybe your parents say you don't have the time, space or money for a dog or a cat. But have you ever tried asking for a Pet Rock?

Gary Dahl's invention, the Pet Rock, went on sale in 1975. Each rock was packaged in a cardboard box. It had a straw nest to keep the rock comfortable and holes to allow for breathing. This was meant as a joke to make the rocks seem like living things.

Pet Rocks sold in the US for $3.95 (£3.06). Gary Dahl became a millionaire!

Pet Rocks also came with an instruction booklet. It explained how to look after and train your pet rock. Suggested tricks included "stay", "roll over" and "play dead".

Does this sound like the perfect pet or does it sound a little crazy to you? Many people thought the idea was funny. More than 1.5 million Pet Rocks were sold!

More low-maintenance pets

If the Pet Rock isn't your style, there are many other low-maintenance pets on the market. The Chia Pet is a small plant that grows in a pot. The pot is shaped like a person, animal or other creature, and the plant grows to become its hair or fur. Another toy pet is the Tamagotchi. It's a handheld virtual reality pet that you can feed, look after and play with. There are even Pillow Pets. These stuffed friends fold out so you can sleep next to them!

Emojis

Can you imagine life without emojis? These images help us share our thoughts and feelings through phones and computers without words. But they didn't exist until 1998.

Emojis were invented in Japan by Shigetaka Kurita. They became popular in the late 2000s. In 2010, they were standardized. This meant that all devices would recognize emojis, no matter which company made them.

Emojis can now be animated, or made to move. These are called animojis. To make an animoji, you need to choose a character. Then, record yourself moving your face to smile, frown, raise your eyebrows or blink. The animoji copies your own movements to show your facial expression.

Shigetaka Kurita poses with a sample of the emojis he invented.

You can even make emojis of yourself!
Just use an app and a phone camera to create
a cartoon version of yourself. You can then
share it in different forms called stickers.

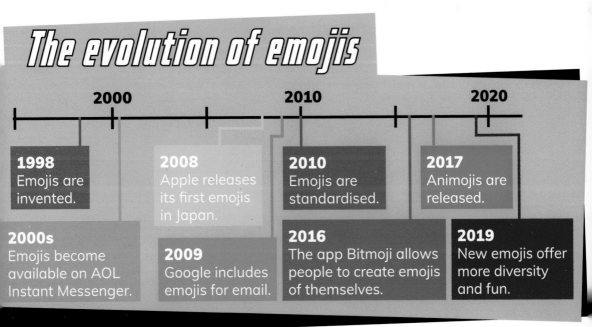

The evolution of emojis

	2000		2010		2020

1998
Emojis are invented.

2008
Apple releases its first emojis in Japan.

2010
Emojis are standardised.

2017
Animojis are released.

2000s
Emojis become available on AOL Instant Messenger.

2009
Google includes emojis for email.

2016
The app Bitmoji allows people to create emojis of themselves.

2019
New emojis offer more diversity and fun.

Wearable blankets

Slankets® and Snuggies® are wearable blankets. They have sleeves to keep your hands free. This allows wearers to do things with a blanket wrapped around them. The Slanket was invented more than 10 years before the Snuggie became available. However, the inventor of the Slanket never obtained a patent for the product, so the idea was fair game. Both wearable blankets continue to be sold.

Wearable blankets keep your hands free while you relax in comfort.

There are so many odd and incredible inventions in this world. But there's always room for more. Think of a problem you have or a need that could be filled. Research what's already available and brainstorm what could be made to solve the problem. With help from an adult, create and test a prototype. Who knows? The next weird invention could be yours!

Fact!

Some inventors hold courses or camps for children. This gives young engineers the chance to create the products they've designed with the help of professionals.

BUT WAIT . . . THERE'S MORE

NOSE STYLUS

A nose stylus is a tool that can be worn on your face. It looks like a long nose or beak. Styluses are like pens for smart devices. They help users write or select items on the screen. The nose stylus is meant to help people use their phones when they only have one hand available. Users can peck out a message, scroll through websites and more.

PING PONG DOOR

Some people like to play ping pong but don't have room for a table. They're in luck! The ping pong door can solve this problem. This invention is a door that opens and closes like most doors. But it can also be folded down. This creates a surface on which table tennis can be played. All you need are two paddles and a ball and you're ready to play!

MAGIC 8 BALL

Do you have questions about life that you'd like answered? The Magic 8 Ball can help! The Magic 8 Ball looks like the 8 ball that's found on pool tables. Inside is liquid and a 20-sided polygon. Each side of the polygon has a different answer. Some answers are positive, some are negative and some are in between.

LED SLIPPERS

LED slippers come with little lights attached to the fronts of them. Weight sensors inside the slippers can tell when someone is wearing them. Light sensors help them know whether or not it's dark. LED slippers can help you find your way around your house in the dark without stubbing your toes.

GLOSSARY

adhesive glue or other substance that makes things stick together

amphibious able to work on land or water

detachable able to be separated or removed from something else

fad something that is very popular for a short time

infringement action that goes against someone's rights

lawsuit legal action or case brought against a person or a group in a court of law

manufacture make something, often with machines

patent legal document giving someone sole rights to make or sell a product

prototype first version of an invention that tests an idea to see if it will work

science fiction stories about the way real or pretend science can change people and the world

stationary not moving

FIND OUT MORE

BOOKS

Great British Inventions (Best of British!), Claire Throp (Raintree, 2019)

Inventors: Incredible Stories of the World's Most Ingenious Inventions, Robert Winston (DK Children, 2020)

What Kids Did: Stories of Kindness and Invention in the Time of Covid-19, Erin Silver (Second Story Press, 2020)

WEBSITES

kids.kiddle.co/Inventor
Find out about more inventors and inventions at this website.

www.littleinventors.org/
Find out how you could be the next famous inventor, with Little Inventors.

www.dkfindout.com/uk/science/amazing-inventions
Learn more about amazing inventions such as the telephone, the wheel and the bicycle.

INDEX